To Mother Nature

Western ghats are one of the world's crucial biodiversity hot spots with many endemic species. This book features animals, birds, and insects found in this region.

Names: Srividhya Lakshmanan (author) |
Akansha Krishnan (illustrator)
Title: Gugulu, The Little Bear Dares
ISBN 9789355788207
Subjects: JUV002000-JUVENILE FICTION-Animals-General |
JUV039220-JUVENILE FICTION-Social Themes-Values & Virtues
Published by: Srividhya Lakshmanan

Visit us online at www.andbooks.in

Please contact at andbooks@gmail.com
Cover Design by Akansha Krishnan
The illustrations in this book were digitally created.

GUGULU

The Little Bear Dares

SRIVIDHYA LAKSHMANAN AKANSHA KRISHNAN

Pretty spots surround the forests of the Western Ghats.

There, under a tree, lives a sloth bear family of three.

It is time to go to school,
and Gugulu wants to be cool.

I want to go all alone,
Gugulu squeaks.

Not until we think you can be on your own, Dad creaks.

Mum asks him to hop on her back
as they walk on the track.
But naughty Gugulu flips and zips.

SWISH! SWOOSH! WHOOSH!

Mum and Dad are nowhere near,
so Gugulu beams and cheers.

Then, he sees a shiny bubble.
He sniffs it and ends up in trouble.

Stay off, you bear. I'm a frog, purple and rare.

She snorts,
and Gugulu darts.

THUD! THUMP! SMASH!

The place is still,
but Gugulu is chill.

He jumps to pull a tail
and hears a wail.

The lion-tailed macaque hoots.
Gugulu scoots.

Mum's calls echo in the air,
but Gugulu does not care.

ZIG! ZAG! ZOOM!

He sprints toward the river
until a screeching voice
gives him a shiver.

Why are you here all alone, bear?

The Nilgiri marten's tone
makes Gugulu groan.

He dashes to the river
and plunges and quivers.

SPLISH-SPLASH-DASH.

Time to cheer,
as there is nothing to fear.

But the flowing water
gives him a jitter.

Mum wobbles on pebbles.

Dad runs faster, worrying about how to get little Gugulu out of the water.

But the flow doesn't slow.

On the other side of the shore,
a leopard's roar scares Gugulu even more.

But the sight of Mum and
Dad lessens his fright.

Soon, Mum and Dad fade in a smoky cloud of dust when a herd of gaurs thump aloud.

The river tide takes Gugulu on a roller coaster ride.

QUAKE! SHAKE! SHIVER!

Mum and Dad watch Gugulu drift away.
While across the shore, a panther waits for his prey.

He slides down her trunk
and lands on the bank with a kerplunk!

DING! DONG! BANG!

TRUNK YOU!

He blows a kiss and bows.

Goes round and round.

He jumps and romps.

He looks at Mum and squeaks and leaps.

HIP-HIP-HOORAY!

Gugulu sees a pangolin whine at her mum about wanting to take a trip alone.

I will be on my own, only when you say I'm grown.

Gugulu says and laughs.

GIGGLE!

BABBLE!

CACKLE!

Sloth Bear
Belongs to - Bear family
Fave food - Ants & termites
Trait: Sense of smell

Purple Frog
Belongs to - Frog family
Fave food - Termites
Trait: Hiding from sight

Lion-tailed Macaque
Belongs to - Monkey family
Fave food - Fruits
Trait: Tall tree climbing

Nilgiri Marten
Belongs to - Marten family
Fave food - Small animals
Trait: Hiding from sight

Indian Roller
Belongs to - Coraciidae family
Fave food - Beetles
Trait: Aerobatics

Meet the

Threatened with extinction

Nilgiri Flycatcher
Belongs to - Flycatcher family
Fave food - Insects
Trait: Hiding from sight

Gaur
Belongs to - Bison family
Fave food - Plants
Trait: Strong fighter

Panther
Belongs to - Cat family
Fave food - Mid-sized animals
Trait: Hiding from sight

Leopard

Belongs to - Cat family
Fave food - Mid-sized animals
Trait: Tree climbing

Southern Birdwing

Belongs to - Swallowtail family
Fave food - Food plants
Trait: A serious flier

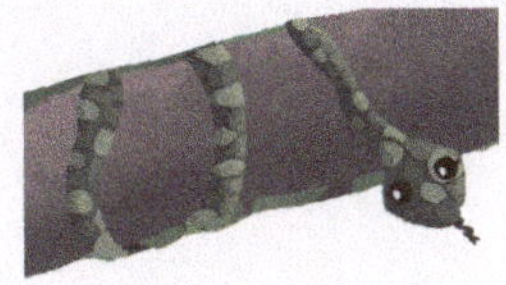

Indian Cobra

Belongs to - Snake family
Fave food - Mice
Trait: Poisonous fangs

tar Cast

★ Native to the Western Ghats

Indian Elephant

Belongs to - Elephant family
Fave food - Legumes
Trait: Sociable and smart

Tamil Yeoman

Belongs to - Nymphalid family
Fave food - Plants
Trait: Glowing wings

Malabar Torrent Dart

Belongs to - Damsel fly family
Fave food - Small insects
Trait: Excellent eye sight

Malabar Giant Squirrel

Belongs to - Squirrel family
Fave food - Fruits
Trait: Tree climbing

Pangolin

Belongs to - Anteater family
Fave food - Ants & termites
Trait: Scaly armor

Can you help me get to school?

Download a free activities book, visit www.andbooks.in.

Other picture books by the author

Thank you for leaving a review.

Join my VIP list for offers & updates.

Sign-up at www.andbooks.in.

Printed at Repro India Ltd.